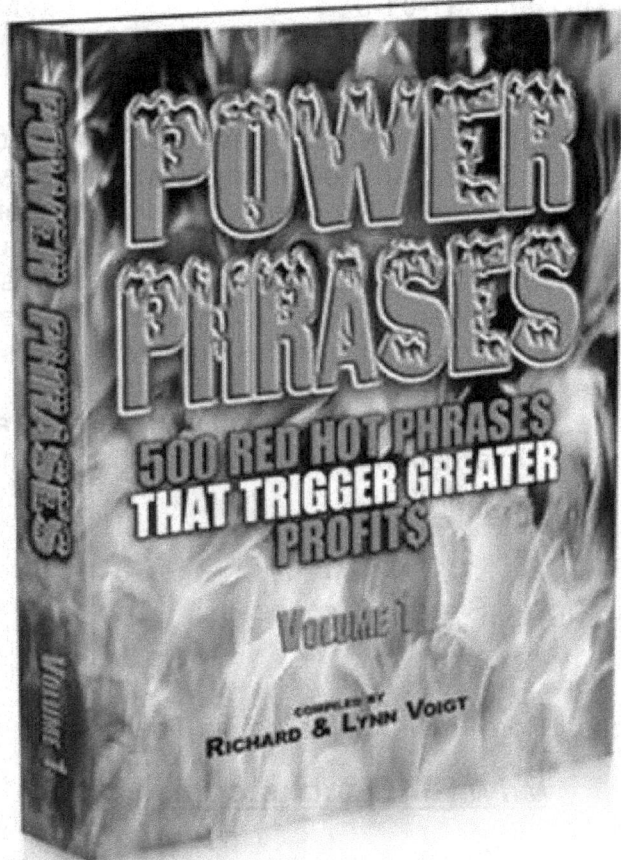

POWER PHRASES – Vol. 1
500 Power Phrases That Trigger Greater Profits

ISBN-13: 978-1-940961-01-9
ISBN-10: 1940961017

First Printing, 2013

Printed in the United States of America

To Access More Powerful Marketing Tools Visit:

www.RIVObooks.com

www.RIVOinc.com

www.WisconsinGarden.com

POWER PHRASES

Volume 1

500 POWER PHRASES THAT TRIGGER GREATER PROFITS

-·|·-•:·*)'''''*·•_ _-·|·_-•**•-·|·-•·*'''''*·•-·|·-

Compiled by

Richard & Lynn Voigt
I.M. Education Specialists

Introduction:

Powerful Phrases, Headlines, Sub Headlines, Slogans, Bullet Points and Interview Sound Bites are perhaps the most powerful marketing tools mankind has ever created. They are the lifeblood behind every business venture are the ultimate secret weapon of Millionaire Marketers.

No matter whether you are introducing or promoting a brand new product, teaching a "How To" skill, building a website, or simply sending an email, using the perfect power phrase is crucial to capturing and holding eyeballs and producing greater marketing profits.

In today's world every word you use has measurable impact. Each word can produce emotional psychological buttons that trigger psychological reactions. Successful advertisers understand that using an effective power phrase is a true art form that turns "wants" into instant gratification "needs." Once artfully triggered, any niche market can instantly create more protifable conversions.

Now it's your turn to personalize this incredible collection of 500 Power Phrases in ways that instantly advance your own effective marketing skills as you create new and power phrases, slogans, presentations, bullet points, or interview sound bites that take you to the next level.

Whether starting or running a small business, writing an ad, coming up with a memorable slogan, making a major corporate presentation, bullet points, creating a video, writing a book, searching for the perfect slogan, teaching a lesson or book report, your creative use of these Power Phrases can capture more eyeballs and produce some amazing rewards quickly turning you into a Marketing Genius. Now, it's your turn to make the magic happen!

POWER PHRASES

Volume 1 – 1- 500

500 Power Phrases That Trigger Greater Profits

Begin Selecting & Customizing Your Perfect Marketing Phrase

1	Negative Advertising Effect
2	Your Future Just Got Closer
3	Activate Your Risk Free Trial Right This Second
4	Know You Can Win This War
5	Why I'll Never Look Back
6	Why Your Focus May Need To Shift To Compete Online
7	Would You Consider Lower Payments
8	What's Your Screen Presence
9	Setting The Stage For Education
10	You Won't Like This
11	No One Really Likes Long Canned Messages
12	The Right Now Sale
13	Are They Looking For Reasons To Delete
14	Things That Kill Business
15	It's Amazing How Well This Works
16	The Real Secrets
17	Ever Wonder What You're Doing Wrong
18	For The Woman Who Needlessly Is Older Than She Looks
19	This Isn't Common Wisdom
20	Your New Account Balance
21	Look What Our Customers Are Saying
22	How To Write Amazing Headlines

6

211	I've Already Added Tons Of Bonuses
212	Turn Your Sub Headlines Into Questions
213	People Are Not Readers So Infotain Them
214	Advertising Now Free And Viral
215	Scratch Everything
216	Will Your Traffic Be There Tomorrow
217	Duel Readership Paths
218	Helping You To Shake Off Anymore Failures
219	Don't Cry To Me If You Miss This One
220	Are You Overrating Your Talents
221	Create A Marketing Fire Online
222	Perfect For Newbies
223	Let Them Make The Sale
224	Hi And Hello
225	Inventive Value Added Provider
226	Tell It Like Your Life Depends Upon It
227	When They See Themselves They Buy
228	Trading Hours Hard Work And Skill For Dollars
229	If You're Not Online You're Screwed
230	Make It Available In All Formats
231	Domain Alarm
232	Sell It As A Product
233	Why Failure Is Important
234	Tried It All And Nothing Still Works
235	Have Someone Interview You
236	Ponder While You Poop
237	Runs On Minimal Input
238	Put Thos Old Tactics To Bed Now
239	Try Something Different
240	Wanted To Get Back To You Quickly
241	To Sue Or Not To Sue
242	Show Up And The Rest Is History
243	Click Here To Activate
244	Giving You The Finest Quality
245	More Than Just Grabbing Their Attention
246	Is This Counter Productive
247	Turn Scanners Into A Readers
248	Avoid Criticism

14

325	Most Definitely It Is The Real Deal
326	Need To Drill Down Even Farther
327	Enter This Code And Save Money
328	Enjoy It Anywhere
329	Save This For Later
330	Just What We've Been Praying For
331	Slick Design
332	Why Fail Like 98% Of Marketers
333	Cash Siphoning Secrets You Were Never Meant To See
334	Charge A Thousand Times More Money
335	Another Major Player Arrived
336	How To Automate Your Marketing
337	Creating New Value
338	Bombarded With Fake Proof And Screenshots
339	Powerhouse Advertising And Profit Sharing
340	Changing At Break Neck Speed
341	You Can Never Have Enough Customers
342	Choosing The Perfect Product
343	Act Now
344	Deliver The Best You Can
345	From Trash To Cash
346	Mobile Experiential Marketing
347	Use Pressure To Prevent Procrastination
348	Find Your Sweet Spot
349	Feelings Reflect Body Posture Thoughts And Words You Use
350	A Lifetime Of Success
351	Referral Promotions
352	For Those On The Move
353	I Must Admit At First I Was Skeptical
354	No Gimmicks No Gadgets Just Hits
355	I'll See You On The Other Side Of The Mouse
356	Success Needs You
357	An Impromptu Workshop
358	Don't Do This Too Quickly
359	Yes These Videos Are Cool
360	Use The First One Soon
361	Years Of Experience
362	Almost Quit Twice

16

401	Free Access Link
402	Don't Keep Making The Same Mistakes
403	Never Be Stuck For Words Again
404	Need A Coat Of Fresh Paint
405	Earners Unite And Grow Together Earn Together
406	Instantly Unlock This Highly Sensitive And Confidential Information
407	Let's Begin Our Venture
408	Look At You
409	Activate Your Free Account Now
410	What Are We In For
411	Improve Your Life
412	Techno Junkie Discovers eGold Mine
413	Where Can You Enjoy This
414	My 2 Hour Work Day
415	One Little Button With Big Results
416	It's Woven Into The Entire Process
417	Feeding On Someone Else's Success
418	Qualities Of A Wealthy Person
419	Communicate It So Simply That They Get It Immediately
420	Is It Appropriate To Dress Conservatively
421	Well Enough Is Enough
422	Who's Your Sponsor
423	Isn't Financial Slavery A Bummer
424	Lure vs. Lull
425	You Truly Deserve The Best
426	With A Solid Foundation Growth Is Exciting
427	Not To Be Continued
428	Never Before Release
429	Profit Plugging Reports
430	Tired Of Worrying About Your Job And Money
431	Tired Of All The Hype
432	The Question I Always Hear
433	Losing vs. Keeping
434	Protect Your Ideas
435	Implications And Actions
436	Soften Your Knees When Standing
437	Rarely Used Ways To Upgrade Your Ad
438	What If People Don't Buy

18

476	Earn While Promoting Your Business
477	When Coaching Is A Big Bonus
478	Create Beauty And Perfection
479	Never Waste Your Time Talking To Brick Walls
480	Enhance Your Sale Videos
481	It's Brand New
482	Why 8 Out Of 10 People Are Stressed Out
483	I Knew This Would Become A Huge Problem
484	They'll Be Back
485	Suffering From Any Of The Above
486	On A Silver Platter
487	Everyone's Got An Opinion
488	The Force That Transforms Everything
489	The Greatest Threat is Obscurity
490	Cut These Anchors Loose
491	Earn Credits Every Time
492	Distraction Interruption And The Art Of Playing Business
493	Top Blunders Common On Most Websites
494	Going From Goal To Goal
495	Focusing On The Big Picture
496	Spread Them Out
497	Delivering The AH-HA Moments
498	Still Full Of Those Pipe Dreams With Nothing To Show
499	All Your Strengths And Passions
500	Brand New Internet Money-Making Ideas That Really Pay

Lynn and I hope that this "Think Tank" volume series of 500 Hot Phrases will helped you clearly paint your dreams, sell your ideas, and market your messages, propelling each of your ideas and projects toward incredible success. Watch for our next Volume!

We truly wish you the very best and look forward to hearing your success stories.

Concluding Thoughts:

Ever success is built upon a preparing a strong foundation, having a clear vision, and taking positive action each and every day. If you've been searching for a new lifestyle, then you'll find this book directive and inspirational. You can open it to any page and let that page help you rethink possibilities, consider new ideas, open new opportunities, and ultimately experience a more successful and fulfilling lifestyle.

Every problem has a solution! Regardless of your current situation or circumstance, know that you have the power and responsibility to redirect your life in any direction you choose. Simply start thinking about and research the kind of lifestyle that truly appeals to your heart. Begin your new journey by learning everything you can about your chosen subject. When you make that commitment, you'll open more unexpected doors to unique opportunities than imagined.

**"Creative Thought Is The Only Reality
Everything Else Is Merely The By-Product Of That Thought."**
- Walter Russell

So why not start thinking **BIGGER? It won't cost you any more.** It all starts by never allowing your current life's situation, environment, or so-called friends to limit your path to a happier, healthier, and successful life. After all, whose life is this?

Make a decision to focus on learning something new each and every day. Begin attracting your ideal lifestyle by doing something you love and enjoy. As difficult as it may be, don't allow money to limit your dreams. Focus on the kind of thoughts that make you feel good. Once you learn how to control your focus, you'll have a great chance to see your dreams take shape. You've finally learn to harness the power you always had within, a Universal Energy stream that flows 365/24/7 in any direction your project your thoughts, Good or Bad. Want proof? The thoughts you currently believe and project reflect the life you're currently living. Therefore, if your life isn't happening, change your thoughts, and change your life. It's something only you can hold, visualize, and project, living your dream come true.

Find yourself a mentor and spend more time with people who truly appreciate, support, and foster your dreams. Life may be short, but the thoughts we hold can make our life wider and more fulfilling.

20

About The Authors:

Richard and Lynn develop creative strategies that paint dreams, sell ideas, & market messages   Together, they present a unique team-approach, working side-by-side, helping clients pursue their passions while sharing their skills and diverse expertise as authors, artists, inventors, entrepreneurs, & Internet marketing education specialists.

Teaching by example, they mentor proven self-publishing services, graphic design, video production, domain acquisition, and marketing research of behalf of their company, RIVO Inc – RIVO Marketing, since 1997. They've created & produced hundreds of videos, self-published dozens of books on a wide variety of topics and created thousands of original works of fine art, while refining their Internet Marketing techniques, mentoring programs, and related business website development.

Their mission is to continually uncover new products and services, test new strategies, and network useful solutions with off and online entrepreneurs, small business owners, writers, local artists, models, teachers, students, and marketing professionals.

Their goal is to help clients create an action plan that discovers and connects the missing pieces of the success puzzle. The goals they foster create multiple streams of income for today's volatile economic climate. Their motto is: "Do the work once and allow the work to create additional streams of income for a lifetime."

Feel free to contact them if you have questions or would like to tap into their talents and expertise. They appreciate your feedback and look forward to hearing your success stories.

Contact:
Richard & Lynn Voigt - RIVO
I. M. Education Specialists

RIVO INC - RIVO Marketing
13720 West Keefe Avenue
Brookfield, Wisconsin 53005 – USA
Email: support@RIVOinc.com
Website: www.RIVObooks.com
Website: www.WisconsinGarden.com

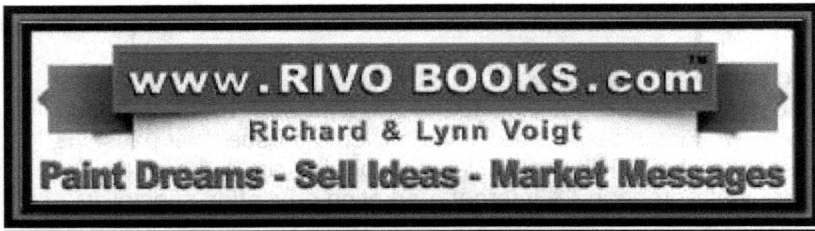

Visit Lynn's Garden: www.WisconsinGarden.com
view hundreds of great garden video blogs Tips

See Richard's Unique Artwork: www.RIVOart.com
view over 3,000 original Fine-Art compositions

Our Book Titles Now Available On Amazon:

THE GOLDEN VAULT OF MOTIVATIONAL QUOTATIONS
Words of Wisdom from The Greatest Minds & Leaders

BABY NAME .ME - 21,400 Names & Nicknames
For Family, Friends, Pets, Natural & Man-Objects

DOODLE DESIGNS Volumes 1-3
For Professionals & Kids Of All Ages
DOODLE DESIGNS – Vol. 1
DOODLE DESIGNS – Vol. 2
DOODLE DESIGNS Coloring Book Vol. 3

Work MORE Accomplish LESS Get FIRED!

ACTION HEADLINES That Drive Emotions – Volumes 1- 6
Paint Dreams, Sell Ideas & Market Your Message
Action Headlines That Drive Emotions Vol. 1
Action Headlines That Drive Emotions Vol. 2
Action Headlines That Drive Emotions Vol. 3
Action Headlines That Drive Emotions Vol. 4
Action Headlines That Drive Emotions Vol. 5
Action Headlines That Drive Emotions Vol. 6

IDIOMS – IDIOMS - IDIOMS
6,450 Popular Expressions That Put Words In Your Mouth

The CLICHÉ BIBLE - 8,400 Clichés For Sports Fanatics
& Lovers Of Popular Expressions

MORE THAN WORDS
5000+ Marketing Phrases That Sell

HYPNOTIC PHRASING
WARNING-This Book Teaches You How To Grab Eyeballs

YOUR RIGHT TO WEALTH
Becoming Wealthy Isn't Hard When You Know How

WI GARDEN – Let's Get Dirty
Our Wisconsin Garden Guide Promoting Delicious, Healthier Home-Grown Fresh Food, With Tools, Tips, & Ideas That Inspire Gardeners!

MONETIZE YOUR SOCIAL LIFE
Earn Extra Income While Having Fun Online

BABY NAMES
21,400 Unique Baby Names & Nicknames

FUNNY HEADLINES vol. 1
3,500 Outrageous Silly Brain Toots

FUNNY HEADLINES vol. 2
3,500 Outrageous Silly Brain Toots

JOBS
10,240 Career Paths That Can Change Your Life!

MONEY WORDS
Powerful Phrases That Million Dollar Copywriters Use To Make Piles Of Cash On Demand!

GARDEN QUOTATIONS
400 Garden Quotes From The Earth To Your Soul

HEADLINE STARTERS
175,000 Words That Paint Dreams, Sell Ideas, And Market Your Message

BABY NAMES
25,350 Baby Names & Nicknames For Your Family Friends & Pets
   697 pages 7,000 Names with Origin & Meaning plus Top 100 Names, And 2,000 Most Popular Names

CURIOUS WORDS
15,800 Words That Expand Your Mind And Change Your Life

INSPIRING THOUGHTS
That Inspire Happiness, Success & A Clearer Understanding Of Life

MARKETING EYEBALLS
100 Ideas That Can Add Unlimited Subscribers To Your Lists

SECOND OF FIVE
My Early Years- From Birth To High School

POWER PHRASES – Individual Volumes 1 - 10
500 Power Phrases That Trigger Greater Profits

POWER PHRASES Pro Edition – Volumes 1-10 (Complete Series)
5000 Power Phrases That Trigger Greater Profits

COMING SOON! – BE THE FIRST TO GRAB YOUR PRO COPY

<u>**POWER PHRASES Pro Edition**</u> Volumes 1-10 (Complete Series)
5000 Power Phrases That Trigger Greater Profits

What do Marketing Millionaires know that you don't? They know how to pull money out of thin air by using their secret language of <u>Power Phrases</u>.

This Pro Edition of <u>5000 Red Hot Power Phrases</u> not only saves you time and money but will help jump-start your creative brain in ways you may have never considered. Simply open this amazing collection to any page and find your perfect power phrase. All it may take is simply adding or replacing ONE word. It's simple, quick, and easy!

1. **Want to create more powerful profitable campaign offers?**
2. **Thinking of revitalizing a more professional business identity?**
3. **Want to update old product or service media advertisements?**
4. **Searching for fresh ideas that could improve sales and profits?**
5. **Looking for brand new ways to create stronger media sales copy?**
6. **Ready to use millionaire strategies advancing you to the next level?**

<u>5000 POWER PHRASES</u> is exclusively for professional Internet Marketers, authors,advertisers, executives, business owners, TV & radio reporters, entrepreneurs, administrators, managers, supervisors, teachers and students who want to find and access unique phrases for marketing slogans, presentation bullet points, and interview sound bites that powerfully paint dreams, sell ideas, and market your message.

Stop wasting valuable time, money, and energy racking your brain for new ideas. Create more profitable power phrase marketing campaigns for all your products, services, slogans, bullet points, and interview sound bites that finally grab and hold people's attention and trigger greater profits?

You now have a very powerful and professional marketing tool in your hand. We are confident that you know how to use it wisely in order to maximize the potential of all your marketing campaigns! Lynn and I **Thank You** for your support and purchase.

CLAIM 500 MORE POWER PHRASES!

Thank you for purchasing this eBook and in doing so we would like to send you **500 More Red Hot Power Phrases for FREE!**

When you post a **positive review of this Book on Amazon Books** under this title you'll receive an additional **500 POWER PHRASES.** Your review may also be sent directly to us.

Your request must be received within 30-days of purchase. Once your positive Book review is posted and verified, simply email the following to **(500@RIVOinc.com)**:

1. Full Name of Purchaser
2. Email address
3. Paypal Invoice Number
4. Copy of your posted Book Review*

Once we receive the above, we'll send you 500 Power Phrases **(PDF)** emailed to the address you provided.

Visit: www.RIVObooks.com for additional volumes as they become available including the Pro Edition of 5000 Red Hot Power Phrases that say what you mean to say and trigger greater profits.

Lynn and I look forward to your written comments and suggestions as we love hearing from each of our readers.

Richard & Lynn Voigt
RIVO Inc – RIVO Marketing
13720 West Keefe Avenue
Brookfield, Wisconsin 53005 USA
Telephone: (262) 783-5335
www.RIVObooks.com

P. S. If you love gardening, catch us on www.WisconsinGarden.com

*NOTE: This offer is valid providing it does not violate the terms of service of the entity with whom you made this purchase. Duplicate or incomplete entries will also not be eligible and this offer is limited to one request per email address. All eligible review submissions become the property of RIVO Inc - RIVO Marketing – RIVO books and may be used as promotional testimonials ads on RIVO Inc websites. This offer may be withdrawn at any time without prior written notice.